WEALTH IN ALL NATIONS

Timeless ideas that will allow anyone to make money anywhere on earth!

Copyright © 2016 by Informal Distribution, LLC.

All Right Reserved.

No part of this publication may be reproduced, distributed, or transmitted in any form or by any means, including photocopying, recording, or other electronic or mechanical methods, or by any information storage and retrieval system without the prior written permission of the publisher, except in the case of very brief quotations embodied in critical reviews and certain other noncommercial uses permitted by copyright law.

INTRO

Dear Reader,

What is the best country in the world to start a business and make millions of dollars?

The answer is yours! There are countries that we automatically associate with having wealth and there are countries that we associate with poverty. And honestly, it will be easier to become rich in one country versus another. However, there is wealth available in all countries and this book is designed to get you started in making money no matter where you happen to be located.

This book is designed to inspire ideas and ways of thinking that will allow you to spot the opportunity for making money that is around you right now using what you already know.

This book is designed to help you make money with the things you see around you every day.

This book is designed to help you make money with the things you hear people talking about every day.

This book is designed to help you make money no matter where you live on planet Earth; no matter the continent or country.

This book is an investment in your financial education that will pay off again and again throughout your life. Read it and began using the information immediately; without drinking the water in your cup you will remain thirsty right? Read it again; you need to drink more than one glass of water, right?

Please, give a review of this book letting us know if you found it useful and how you plan to apply the information provided.

May Almighty God bless your purchase of this book and all your efforts to be a success in life!

Table of Contents

INTRO

Chapter 1

Borrow Heavily From Existing Products&Services

Chapter 2

Combine two businesses into One in order to Create a Market Opening

Chapter 3

Begin With A Problem In Mind

Chapter 4

Recognize A Hot Trend & Ride The Wave

Chapter 5

Study Existing Products & Services and Explore Ways to Improve Function

Chapter 6

"Think of Ways to Streamline a Customer's Activities"

Chapter 7

Adapt Product or Service to Meet Customer's Needs In A Different Way

Chapter 8

Expand Market for Product/Service

Chapter 9

Take Existing Products/Services and Make Them "Green"

Chapter 10

Keep An Eye On Emerging Technologies

CHAPTER 1
BORROW HEAVILY FROM EXISTING PRODUCTS&SERVICES

In order to start a successful business, you don't have to start from scratch. One of the best things you can do is look around you and see what is already working for someone else. The simple truth is, if it works for them, it will work for you. Fast food businesses do it all the time. First came McDonald's, then Burger King, Wendy's, and so on and on. Get the point?

You don't have to reinvent the wheel in order to make lots of money. Many people make the mistake of trying to come up with something no one has seen before. That is actually the hardest and last thing you should ever do. First, people are creatures of habit and go with what they know. So, if you want some of their money to get into your pocket you should give them something they are familiar with; or reminds them of something that they are familiar with in some way.

Grab a piece of paper and a pen or pencil to write with. You are going to use this to jot down some ideas. I always find, that writing something down makes it more real to you and makes it easier to visualize.

Write down these things:

What sort of business do you want to start?

Do you know how to run this kind of business?

Can you learn to run this kind of business?

Would this be a good business where you are located or will you open it somewhere else?

Are there too many businesses like this where I am now?

Where do people where I live spend their money now?

Can I start a business that works for other businesses?

How much money would it take to start this business?

Can I afford to put my money into this business?

Is there a large enough market to support this business?

Will I operate the business full time or part time?

This list is not exhaustive but these are some of the things you want to consider when choosing any business that you aim to build your wealth with.

If there are already many of the same type of businesses where you would like to start your business, the chances that you will succeed are slim to none. But, that is not always the case. In large cities, you may find several of the same type of businesses surviving next door to each other or across the street from each other. The more people in a given area the greater chance similar competing businesses have of making money.

However, if you choose a business that has the **least** amount of competition, you give yourself the greatest chance of success. Competing businesses in the same market have to share one pie and there are only so many slices of pie. Your goal is to get as many slices of pie that you can. Choosing a business with the least amount of competition in a chosen market gives you the greatest chance of getting more slices of pie; and in this case, slices of pie equals money!

Some businesses, like car dealerships, **can't** even open up a store in certain areas if the area doesn't have a high enough population to support that business. Are you in an area with a small population? Are there certain businesses that you have to drive to the "big city" to shop at? Can you start a business that will provide that service to your community? Drive around in that city and see what types of businesses are available. Which one would work best for you in your situation using the questions above.

Even if you can't provide all the services that the big city businesses offer, provide a service that you can do well. Your neighbors and others in your community would definitely prefer to use something close by to something far away if you are professional and courteous.

And since you would be the only business providing this service in this market, you'll have the whole pie to yourself! (at least in the beginning)

If you are in a big city, is there a business that is not represented in your neighborhood?

Can you take an idea/service being provided on the other side of town and make it available to yours?

Tap a market that others have neglected. And being the first to address this need you will have the whole pie to yourself. That is until competition sets up shop!

You can also start a business that is not in your country.

Have you traveled to another country?

What businesses did you see there for the first time?

Would any of them be good in your country for building wealth using the questions above?

Nowadays, you don't even have to travel to different countries to see what is available there. Use the internet to research different places/locations and learn about them:

What do they do for fun?

What do they eat?

How do they dress?

These are some of the things that you can use to your business advantage. Borrow from them the ideas that will make you rich where you are.

The name of the game is wealth and finding ways to build it. By finding ways to borrow the products and services of others, you put yourself on the fast track to do so. You won't necessarily get wealthy overnight; but you will get wealthy faster using what already exists then totally starting from scratch.

CHAPTER 2
COMBINE TWO BUSINESSES INTO ONE IN ORDER TO CREATE A MARKET OPENING

Being a businessman means always thinking about how to expand your profits. Expanding the business and your profits is something you always strive to do. It's not always easy to accomplish.

Sometimes it might seem to be impossible. You can overcome this hurdle by combining two businesses and opening a new market for yourself.

There's always the option of combining two business for the purpose of creating a new market opening; to unite two different target markets, enlarging the number of customers who use your business and the size of each customer's purchase. This will help you earn much more wealth for you and your family.

The idea is to stand out among the competition and establish yourself as the go to business for this service/product. By providing a double-service/product, you are able to create a new market.

When you offer a single service and or product, you may or may not have a lot of competition. Once you combine two or more services, your competition narrows. This allows you to provide a unique combination of services that will be hard for your competition to match; unless they begin to copy what you are doing.

By staying in constant communication with your customers and treating each one as a valuable source of information, you will know what other products/services they need that they aren't buying from you presently. Then add those products services/products within your own business!

Your income stream will grow from the same river. You will always make a decent living just from providing what people are already buying; or by introducing them to **new products** that people are buying elsewhere but haven't had a chance to locally.

And by having a good relationship with your customers, you can always change the mix of products/services you offer to capture more income for yourself and your family.

You can apply this method to almost any type of business! The thing is to be smart about which type of mix you're putting together.

They have to complement each other wisely, for the benefit of your customers.

Some products/services go hand in hand with others; for instance, ketchup with French fries.

Find the product/service that goes together with what you already sell in the course of business and you can't lose; unless your prices are higher than your competitors!

Do your homework and always remain competitive!

The idea is to create a smart combination that is appealing to your target audience while providing a higher than normal income for you.

Let's see some examples of different markets and how two businesses can be joined into one:

Cleaning services and dog-walkers - People who lack the time to clean their house might also not have enough spare time to walk their dog (especially in the mornings, which are working hours). By adding this service in addition to the cleaning, you have just given yourself extra income from the same customer who would otherwise have hired someone else.

Indoor Playground For Busy Mothers – Young mothers usually need a break from home, and their babies also need a safe place away from home to experience and play in.

Baby playgrounds, placed in neighborhoods populated by young families, can be a great source of income.

Providing additional services will only increase foot traffic to the business.

You will in effect be providing a safe environment for parents and their children; where they can take care of some errands and have a refreshment without worrying about their children.

This is a service/product the right customers will gladly pay for.

Vegan restaurant and organic supermarket – This combination is aimed at a growing market of health-conscious people. With the right mix of products and services, they will visit you daily; if not for dining, then for shopping or the opportunity they will have to socialize with others who share the same gastric values.

Most vegans are socially conscious about several issues including:

The environment, animals' rights and their own health.

You will be able to provide them with delicious organic products to purchase on one hand; and on the other hand you can provide them with an environment to enjoy a healthy meal made from these same ingredients important to their lifestyle.

Finding and serving a niche like this will allow you to become a second home for a specific group of people and enjoy HUGE profits!

Musical instruments plus tutoring services – You can create a name for yourself by creating a one stop environment that caters to music lovers. Your store can have separate areas for tutoring and practicing for which you can charge separate fees.

Hire salesmen/tutors who play the instruments you sell; opening up a natural secondary sale from the same customer. for tutoring lessons sold in addition to the instrument.

These salesman/tutors will give your shop and products an aura of first hand expertise that the internet can't compete with.

You may also expand *your* products and services to the internet offering lessons online!

Always do your own research and plan carefully.

Make the most of what you do know; and build on your relationships with customers and suppliers who may provide you with additional firsthand information you can get nowhere else.

In this way, you will be able to successfully combine two or more businesses into one.

CHAPTER 3
BEGIN WITH A PROBLEM IN MIND

In order to start a successful business, you need only to find a way to fix a problem.

There are billions of dollars made every day addressing the most basic problems facing all humans on planet earth:

food, shelter, clothing, education, healthcare, transportation, entertainment, and security.

What can you think of that would fit into this category?

You can make millions for yourself by addressing an important area of concern wherever you live.

Choose something that few people have to deal with and you will make small profits.

Find something that many people have to deal with and you will make large profits.

The best way to identify a profitable problem is to use your life and activities as a starting point.

Have you thought about how a product or item you use on a daily basis can be better than it is now?

Can you change it's shape, purpose, function or price?

Finding these solutions is where the profits are to be had and where you begin to build wealth for yourself.

In Saudi Arabia they use snowplows; not to plow snow, but to push sand out of roads and driveways.

Can you find a new way to use a snow plow? If not a snow plow then what?

There are plenty of products that can be used for purposes different than their intended ones.

Think about the ones that you can use that no one else has thought of already. Or use something that others are already using far away but not in your locality.

In the first chapter we talked about studying other countries and cultures in order to find ideas that you can borrow from them. What problems do they face on a regular basis?

Some countries face typhoons and earthquakes on a regular basis and you may not. How do they deal with these issues? What kind of businesses arise to deal with the rebuilding process?

Can you start this type of business and provide such a service where you are at? Or, can you provide the service that people need in these countries by moving there?

Is there a problem that is new to where you live that people in other places have been dealing with for a long time? How did businesses deal with this problem, and profit from it, there?

Business people are leaders who take the initiative where they are to address the problems of people in their community.

That is you! This is why you are reading this book right?

Open your eyes to what is happening around you and your customers/neighbors. Only you can identify areas that would be profitable to your business in your community.

If you need to find out more information, do you know where to go?

The internet is a fantastic tool to gather information if there are no local libraries available.

If you do have a local library, you can do in depth research that may not be possible on the internet. Searching databases made open to the public will lead you to providers of tools and resources you may need to properly set up and run your business.

And more importantly, these will help you to research the business you are planning to start and give you enough data to know whether the business is worth the effort to invest the time and funds into in the first place.

Use the Google search engine and type in free databases and see what pops up. If you need to narrow down the search, use "parentheses" and choose words more closely related to the subject you are trying to research; such as "pay toilets", "businesses under $1,000.00", "importing food" or "exporting food", etc…

You must be proactive and find things that may or may not be apparent. Some things will be easy to spot, but others may take some creative thinking to identify.

Deliberately build a plan of action for yourself:

How can you solve this problem? Is it worth solving? Is there enough money in it to build a business around it? Do you have enough information about the problem to appropriately solve it?

The name of the game is wealth and finding ways to build it. By finding ways to solve the problems of others you put yourself on the fast track to actually build the wealth you always wanted for you and your family.

You won't necessarily get wealthy overnight; but you **will** get wealthy when you start a business that solves a problem that exists for a large number of people.

CHAPTER 4
RECOGNIZE A HOT TREND & RIDE THE WAVE

In order to start a successful business, you can recognize a hot trend & ride the wave.

Many ideas are on their way to becoming more popular/profitable than they are right now. The earlier you find and identify these trends, the easier it will be for you to capitalize on these trends and build wealth for you and your family.

There are different trends for different categories. There are trends related to men, there are trends related to women. There are trends related to children, technology, pets, home ownership, car ownership, recycling, health, energy, war, weapons, metals, farming, mining; the list is limitless.

Everything you see in this world is increasing or decreasing; changing and being changed in some way. By taking the time to find information related to a particular subject, then studying it thoroughly, you can find plenty of ways to make money using this information in a profitable way.

The key to making lots of money recognizing trends is to have the best information possible. The most honest and varied information you can get your hands and eyes on will allow you to best prepare yourself for how you to profit from the trend.

A lot of respectable business magazines, newspapers and books provide information on long term economic indicators that will have consequences for months or years to come. Find the ones most useful to you locally.

Different websites also provide financial information in the form of articles, videos and graphs which allow the viewer/reader to use expert analysis to make financial decisions. Find this information. Use this information.

Libraries are full of information; many have business sections with staff that will assist you. They often have local and national databases that you can access to gather any statistics you may need to gauge the truthfulness of information you have already gathered at his point. Or, they can be used as a starting point to give you direction on where you should focus your research next.

You always have to be careful to make sure that the information you receive is neutral and truthful. Many periodicals, websites and the various articles you may read are neither neutral or truthful.

Many times they are actually sales pitches meant to sway the reader to use a certain product or invest in certain stocks or funds by a writer that stands to profit from getting you to believe and act on their article. So, be careful! Not all information is good information and many times it is more than bad, it is simply a lie.

Despite the best information, any attempts to predict the future will always fall short of the reality. However, when you use the best information available at the time and mentally prepare and allow a range below and above the trend's target area, you will always win.

As a matter of fact, when you are conservative in your estimates and prepare for the worst case scenario you show that you are smarter than most people.

Most people always see the bright side of any information they receive. They believe they will always hit the home run; that they will have tons of people coming to their business spending lots of money as soon as they open for business. Don't be that dumb.

You should know that even the biggest and successful businesses that you know of now almost failed when they first started. Yours likely will too. By preparing yourself for lean times when you start your business, you will expect to save money every step of the way.

You won't be disappointed if people don't come in flocks to your business right away; you will know that it may take weeks, months or even years before you make your fortune.

The important thing is to do your research using the best available information, figure out how best to profit from this information, define clearly how you will run this business profitably; not spending more money than necessary to start this business, and how would this business survive under the worst case scenario.

Another tidbit on the information you gather; you don't want it to be based on trends that will take many years to develop. You want information no further out than a year or two.

Anything further than that,(and even two years may be too long for some businesses), it just won't be any good to you. There is simply no way to know what will happen so far into the future.

Make note of further predictions, and as the years pass question whether earlier predictions were right or wrong. Base your action on the current proven trend, not the one predicted for the future.

CHAPTER 5
STUDY EXISTING PRODUCTS & SERVICES AND EXPLORE WAYS TO IMPROVE FUNCTION

There are all kinds of business around you; If you look outside, you might see various stores offering food, home supplies, clothes, cosmetics, laundry services, restaurants and cafes, bookstores and many more.

You can go further and think of different private service providers; home cleaning, private shoppers, dog walkers, even babysitting can be a real business!

These few examples can be something you can take, do better, and make a living with to support you and your family. You have to find an unfulfilled need in the potential customers around you; address it, by improving on the products and services that currently exist.

If you don't find any profitable ideas right away – keep looking around and try to come up with different business models that are suitable for your environment.

If you live close to a tourist attraction, use this to your advantage. Do you have many lonely people in your area who use various dating services? You can that fact to create a new type of dating club.

Keep an open mind and come up with a few ideas until you find the one that you understand well enough to start making money with.

Whenever you have questions, jump online first. It's a good source of research material that is cheap and fast. However, you always want to verify any information you may find to check it's truthfulness and to get a second opinion.

Remember, just because you find it online doesn't make it a fact!

Also, take some of the businesses you see around you and make a checklist of what equipment you might need in order to start out.

If you're opening a shop, you'll have to rent a place, buy insurance, hire a cashier, contact suppliers, open a bank account, get licenses to sell specific types of products etc.

If you want to open a bakery, you'll need to have a commercial kitchen, inspections by the local health department, supplies (among a long list of other things).

Do people pay to store property in self-storage facilities where you live? Can you find a way to profit from this by changing the size and location of where items are stored. Could you possibly convert an old warehouse to a private storage facility? In certain areas this idea would get no response; in another area, it may be just what the market needs.

Everywhere there's a need; your job is to find it.

After making some points online, it's time to get real and go look at what's out there. This is only applicable if your business is meant to be a "brick and mortar" one. It's good to learn the business firsthand by touching and using the equipment associated with that particular business.

You may find it too noisy, stinky, dirty, or too physically demanding. Many entrepreneurs are picking online business these days (being an affiliate, Amazon seller, designer or programmer, etc.) but it's up to you and your skills.

Always do a thorough investigation into any investment you plan to make of time, cash and your **reputation** into any business. You have to consider all options, including the worst-case scenarios.

Choose your location wisely; make sure the target audience can get to your location, as well as capture the attention of people who usually walk nearby. The choice of location has to be logical and go hand in hand with your choice of business.

After getting a better understanding of your own capabilities and desires, it's time to think about your target audience. You need to have a clear and realistic vision:

Who are your customers\users? What is their social status? Age group? Gender? What main interests they might have? And where and how are their needs being currently met and by whom?

Knowing your market extremely well will determine your success. You may need to focus your advertising to a small niche in large markets to find success.

Finding a small underserved niche is actually the best market to address for two beautiful reasons.

1. You want have much competition starting off because the nice is too small for larger business to serve well.

2. Many times people will pay more for items that they have previously not been offered to them; so will have higher margins on the products/services you sell to this niche.

The most certain way of finding your own voice in the business world is to find something extra ordinary.

If we're talking about a food business – you can come up with special meal idea or combine different approaches, cuisines, or invent your own appetizer or sauce (remember KFC – it was started to specialize in one dish served right).

Find an idea that works for you. Provide your customers with a product/service that they need for a price you both can live with. Make sure that they are happy with your service/products and constantly seek to improve your offerings and your profits.

This system will allow you to create a profitable working routine. If it's a service of any kind, you can win by going the extra mile, providing personal approach, investing in a website with an online shop, delivery service and additional services according to the needs of your target audience.

Never stop finding ways to improve on existing services and products!

CHAPTER 6
"THINK OF WAYS TO STREAMLINE A CUSTOMER'S ACTIVITIES"

Starting up a business and managing it properly requires a lot of knowledge, effort and innovation. Increasing the customer base is one of the foremost priorities of any business organization as it is their main source of revenue.

Your business can aim to serve other businesses and organizations by helping them streamline activities that are a part of their operation.

Streamlining focuses on improving the efficiency of processes by simplifying or reducing the unnecessary steps using modern management techniques and approaches.

Define your customer base; know what businesses and industries are a good fit for your skill set. If you have years of experience working with various businesses in numerous industries, then you should really be able to put those skills to use in a most profitable way immediately.

If you have experience or training in one area, then obviously your efforts, at least initially should be aimed to serve that particular field/industry.

This is a really lucrative market which will always have a strong demand; especially when the economy is bad. This is a field that pays well as it adds to your customer's bottom line almost immediately; and it continues to pay dividends to them years down the road.

The hardest part of this type of business is landing the contract to do the work in the first place.

You should know and understand your competition well. What are they charging for the service you plan to offer? How have they been successful landing contracts? What is their method of operation?

Eliminating errors they have made and improving your service accuracy is a must to distinguish yourself and establish your reputation.

If your business is able to deliver a good product right the first time, this will save customers' time and costs.

Identifying bottlenecks (areas that delay operations) is very important. Your job is to eliminate mistakes your customer is making. Whether it is their supply chain, product quality, delivery time, distribution network; getting things right after implementing your recommendations is the objective.

If you have an employee who is specialized in several fields, it can be a very good advantage to your business as he is capable of providing expertise in several areas of business.

Hiring multi skilled employees will enable you to cover more industries and earn greater profits. This may allow you to use your time looking for more contracts and dealing with customer service issues. This will eliminate delays and misunderstandings and will lead to the streamlining of your business as well.

Customers should always be treated in a friendly manner as he is the source of income for your business. Even and especially when they are upset and venting their anger and frustration! I if you are capable of making your customers feel relaxed when interacting with your business, you will establish trust, build up a solid well-earned reputation that you to grow wealth for you and your family.

A real customer oriented business entity will implement corrective actions to improve their processes based on customer feedback they receive. This will help to boost sales by identifying real customer needs and taking the necessary actions to improve customer service.

Making customer service a priority in your business should be a no brainer. You will be in close contact with your customer on a day to day basis and being let in on their private operations; they need to trust and like you for them to open up to you in this way!

Being responsive to all their concerns, especially privacy, in and outside of their operations will help you reach a higher level of customer satisfaction.

In this case we can identify 3 factors that will support to streamline your service to customers. Those are:

1.Convenience – Making the process as simple and stress free as possible for your client.

2.Speed- A timely approach allows you to do your job without inconveniencing the customer or their operations.

3.Effectiveness-The customer receives exactly what they want from their interaction with your business.

Extended hours of operation will provide your customers more convenience and increase their satisfaction.

A well planned strategy should be implemented to actively guide your activities by anticipating client responses and offering solutions in a proactive way to create a mutually beneficial outcome for the both parties.

CHAPTER 7
ADAPT PRODUCT OR SERVICE TO MEET CUSTOMER'S NEEDS IN A DIFFERENT WAY

In order to provide a truly valuable service to your customer which will benefit them at every turn, a good business person will attempt to adapt products or service to meet customer's needs in a different way.

There is no one single way to do this and it will take intelligence on your part to know your customer personally and intimately.

For instance, in Saudi Arabia snowplows are used to move large amounts of sand from drive ways and roadways after sandstorms; somebody came up with the idea to sell snowplows for this purpose after seeing the problem and coming up with a solution using a product made for another purpose. You should always aim to do the same thing.

No matter what your main business is, your customers are people who will do business regularly with someone they can trust and who they can respect. By keeping yourself in tune to them as an individual, and not just as a customer, people will feel special whenever they have dealings with you.

People like to feel special; and knowing that they can trust your advice in areas outside of your normal business dealings will increase their confidence in you. This means they will be less likely to go to other competitors who are offering the same service or products as you.

You should remember conversations you have with you customers and after they are gone, perhaps later that night, research a way to address a problem they discussed with you. Make this a regular pattern and keep notes on what you find while researching these particular needs.

More customers will eventually have this problem if they don't currently. By keeping notes, you can organize information to be filed for later use or built upon with further study or new information.

This information may be the basis of an entirely new business which may be more profitable than your current source or may be an addition which may help you build greater wealth for you and your family.

Make an effort to gather information from your customers through surveys. They don't have to be exhaustive or expensive in nature. They can be informal; by simply saying," I'm taking a survey of my customers and I'd like to ask you a few questions." Then simply write down the main issue or answer you received from them.

Find out what is important to them. Find out what is most on their mind these days. What worries them. Things they need to do, but haven't been able to accomplish for one reason or another. Then find a way to help your customer by addressing that issue; especially an issue that many people share because that is where you will make the most money for your business. The biggest businesses address the biggest problems.

Customer retention is key to building a business and making it more profitable. Especially if you are a consultant to other businesses. Many people make a living helping businesses find answers to their problems.

Not necessarily fixing the problem themselves but by finding an answer or choice of options for their customers with both positive and negative information regarding the selections which will enable them to make the best possible decision based on your research.

Big businesses hire expensive firms to do this for them. But mid-size and smaller businesses may hire a freelance consultant (you) to work on this problem for them. There are no particular licenses, certificates or degrees needed for most businesses. However, certain areas such as law and medicine would require specific education in that field. Other fields may also require local permits or certificates. Be aware of all laws in your area regarding the business you are conducting.

Obviously, being a thorough investigator and meticulous gatherer of pertinent information is important. But, having the ability to concisely and effectively communicate your findings to your client in a way that allows them to fully understand the issue and the best decision to make based on your work is priceless. It will not only lead to repeat business but referrals which will give you the ability to build wealth for yourself and your family.

Remember, profits aren't everything they are the only thing!

You are not in business for the smiles and giggles; you have to eat food paid for in cash. Your home, car and clothing is paid for in cash. So, getting paid for your work is important.

Use the internet, business magazines and newspapers and trade journal to find out the prices for various services and products worldwide and compare them to local prices.

Sometimes you can capitalize on price differences. For instance, you may be able to purchase a product cheaper online and have it drop shipped to your business at a price cheaper than the competition.

Or you may know someone who provides a service or product locally cheaper than somewhere else. You could purchase the service/product from him after securing the sale and make a profit for simply being the middleman. You can do this on behalf of yourself or other businesses, or both! You decide what is sustainable and most profitable in the long run for you.

Always aim for fast, efficient and accurate service and products.

If you can't offer high quality service and products at a competitive price, then offer high quality service and products at a high price! Never sell your customer short by offering the second rate service or products. If they want and ask for second rate products, then by all means sell them those.

But, do so by letting them know in advance what they are getting compared to the higher quality items. Never be known as the person who has second rate service or products.

You may never be able to shake that image in the mind of your customers later when you decide to step up your quality to the higher priced items. In their minds, you will always be second rate.

So, remember that there are many ways to adapt products and services to meet your customer's needs in a different way but ALWAYS make sure they are top notch products and services!

CHAPTER 8
EXPAND MARKET FOR PRODUCT/SERVICE

A market has been defined in many ways and includes," a geographical area of demand for commodities." This can, and most often does, include people inside or outside a particular geographical area.

The use of modern methods of communication in combination with the world wide web means that you can make contact with someone today who you would otherwise never meet your entire life. The opposite is also true; they can make contact with you!

So, how can you expand your market for your product or service? First, you need to know who buys from you and why they do so.

Is it because of proximity? Are they able to buy your product because they have a higher income than average? Or do they buy from you because they have an average or below average income?

You must know your customers thoroughly; through every conceivable means that do not cross ethical lines you should know the buying habits of your customers. The reason?

That individual is part of a larger body of customers, near and far. Even in areas with a smaller population, the buying characteristics in your locality is found throughout the world. And the more you know about that type of personality/character, you can find it or have a good idea of where to find it anywhere on earth.

To do this effectively, you need to analyze customer data. This may be through conversations, surveys, internet research, or personal research using tools available to you locally.

Many times government offices can provide information on population trends, demographic breakdowns of the population, investments, sales figures and trends.

Trade organizations also may provide detailed information regarding their particular field in a detailed manner not found elsewhere.

In the U.S., local libraries are a fantastic tool to access information free of charge to those on a budget.

Understanding a little psychology would also be beneficial. There are certain needs we all have depending on our personality types.

Learning the difference in personalities you come across and the motivations behind those personalities gives you an edge that can repeat itself with every individual of that personality type.

They will be prone to gather at certain places, to engage in certain activities, to find pleasure in particular entertainment; once you know this you can begin to expand your market to find this "individual" anywhere on planet earth.

Know thy self, first!

The best business is operated by a person who understands human nature. The better you understand you, the better you will understand your customer.

The simple reason is this; every person on earth has the same needs. We are the same as those we meet; we are just prone to different likes and dislikes, different pleasures and boredoms. Know these in yourself thoroughly first. Then, whenever you meet someone, your customer or potential customer, try to find yourself in this person.

Think about what it would take you in your own mind to BE this person. Once you come to a good grasp of the customer who regularly buys from you and you see yourself in this person consistently, you will become him in a way that allows you to find him wherever he might be because you have only to think about where YOU might be found.

In any country on planet earth.

You may have to learn something about the cultural environments in different countries, and also their particular ways of doing business. But, once you get past the societal masks we must wear due to forced conformity, there is the individual personality seeking your product/service.

This may require you to formulate a strategy to reach this personality type.

Take a pen and paper and write down what you know about this customer. Their motivations. Their needs. How your product/service meets their needs. How you can get them to understand that your product/service meets those needs. What is the best way for you to communicate how your product/service meets those needs.

Always start with those close to you and begin to expand from there. Though, if you are technically proficient, you may be able to do business with a customer you have never met locally. Sometimes, because of societal norms or other taboos, you may not be able to sell your product/service locally where you live. You may have to access your customer solely through technology.

In that case you will have to understand your situation from a legal standpoint locally and begin from there. I do not encourage anyone to be involved in illegal activities that may destroy themselves or their family. But, if you have the ability to sell something in another country that is totally legal there and does not require you to violate the laws of the land where you live, then go for it!

Social media makes this possible by helping you to establish links with people all over the world. While most people use these for fun, emotional, or personal reasons, you should do so with an eye for business.

Find individuals where you aim to do business and chat with them extensively. Learn all you can about their culture and how to access it from where you are.

Again, your product/service is needed by people all over the world, but they may not engage in the same types of activities in different cultures.

They may have more or less money to buy your product/service depending on the country they are in. Knowing these particulars will allow you to expand your market with intelligence and success.

CHAPTER 9
TAKE EXISTING PRODUCTS/SERVICES AND MAKE THEM "GREEN"

At this time in human history, we have finally woke up to the fact that there are finite resources on planet earth.

Making the most of what materials we have and reducing the use of the harmful ones has become a cause that everyone can agree on. From celebrities to politicians, business owner and consumer benefit when we do our part to respect nature and our environment.

This is sometimes called the "green" movement.

What does it mean to make a product "green"?

Green products have been defined in many ways. They can be considered as products/services that have less of a negative environmental impact; or are less detrimental to human health and the environment than the traditional product equivalent.

They have also been defined as making current products more efficient or more durable. The idea being that the longer you use something, the longer it stays out of the garbage and the landfill. And the longer you use something, you don't have to replace it with another product; meaning a reduction in the use of materials in the production process.

You can profit from this trend, which will only grow in importance as humanity continues to grow in numbers, in a number of ways. If you are already in business offering a product/service to customers currently, you can add environmentally friendly products/services as an alternative to a current product being offered.

Many people will pay more for such products in order to do "their part" to help the environment. Sometimes, the "green" product will be cheaper for you to purchase or make yourself but can be priced the same as conventional product leading to higher profit margins.

You may decide, depending on your customer base and their interest in nature and the environment, to sell nothing but "green" products/services. This can give you an edge in comparison to other businesses if you are the first to make this issue a cause at the heart of your business.

Many people will feel that doing business with you is helping a good cause and will give them some status for being intelligent enough to care about such matters.

It will also serve as great advertising for your business since many people now stake their names and reputations, to support businesses which champion this popular cause.

You should always do your homework before making any business decision and take your time to understand your customer's attitudes about such matters. Any cause, no matter how noble, is not worth losing your business reputation for!

Investigate how you could implement a "green" program; what it would mean for you. Are there ways to offer "green" alternatives and traditional products/services? Are there reliable products/services locally that fit the bill that are of high quality?

If not can you make such products yourself?

There are many companies that specialize in "green" products which have a presence on the internet. You can shop between various manufacturers and find the most profitable products/services just right for your customers locally.

By doing some research online, you will also find many recipes for "green" products which you may be able to make yourself cheaply.

Depending on your level of competence you can make your own product, purchase containers and print professional labels and start manufacturing your own product which will be as good or better than offerings currently being sold.

The products can be low tech to high tech depending on your budget. From appliances to household cleaning products; laptop cases to self-adjusting thermostats.

What you will be able to sell is limited only by your ability to find customers.

Do an internet search for the top 100 green products to get an idea of the possibilities of products available for sale. Pick a list of the top products you decide would be good for your customers and establish contact with the manufacturer/supplier and gather all the information you need to make an intelligent decision.

You can also find ways to address environmental issues locally which will cost you little but will pay off big financially and/or positively for your business. Much of what people throw away and send to the landfill can be re-used.

For instance, food scraps and other organic materials can be used to produce compost. (research compost businesses online)

By setting up an area where food businesses and local people can 'throw away' such material you can gather free ingredients which can be later sold to farmers and others who want humus to grow vegetables, herbs, flowers or to use in landscaping their lawns.

You could also set up a recycling area for other materials which have value.

Paper, glass, batteries, used oil (used in cars and for cooking), metals of all sorts can be re-used. Do your research and contact business in your area or those that are closest in proximity to you that would buy such materials and in what amounts.

Usually, they buy large amounts so you may need a considerable area to store these materials in an organized way for possibly months at a time before they would be sold to a buyer. Again, the more research you do, the better your decision will be.

Many times government regulations are in place to keep many of these harmful materials out of the ground so that they do not leach into our groundwater and wind up poisoning us years later.

So, having a recycling center close to where they live would serve your community good in many ways. Local officials may even make it mandatory for people to use your center; meaning you will have many customers giving you a free product that you can turn around and sell. Can it get any better than that?

There are so many things that can be done in this area that this chapter is not even touching the tip of the iceberg. This is an area that will continue to be profitable into the future for many years to come.

It is not a fad or fashion; this is a worldwide problem with a worldwide solution and there will always be room for the smart business owner to make a few (or many) dollars.

Depending on your talents, connections, the size of your business and other factors, this may or may not be applicable for you.

However, in the grand scheme of things, it is truly a way to gain wealth in any nation on earth!

CHAPTER 10
KEEP AN EYE ON EMERGING TECHNOLOGIES

Wealth In All Nations aims to help the reader brainstorm ideas for new income streams; we do not recommend a particular business, market, business structure or geographic location.

Some of what has been discussed will apply to certain areas more than others.

With that being said, where there is a will there is a way!

The one thing that is more important than anything else is making the most of your intelligence!

Increasing your knowledge at every turn and always improving how you do things. This will be your biggest edge in gaining wealth for you and your family. Keeping an eye on emerging technologies then certainly makes sense.

Different businesses use different levels of technology; some more, some less. Some companies need the latest computer technology to operate and others may use notepads and a calculator.

Sometimes you may find that an upgrade does not make your business more efficient than the former version. Or it may not pay to buy a particular piece of equipment because it does not add to your bottom line.

You must always weigh the pros and cons of any purchase and make the most of your financial budget.

However, you need to do your homework about what equipment/technology is available which might aid your business and make it more profitable. Possibly a gadget used in a completely different field may help your shop to operate more smoothly and at a faster pace than before; increasing your profits dramatically.

In order to stay at the top of your game, you need to be flexible. This will allow you to grow and respond to changes in the market as the need arises.

You also don't need to be an expert in any one particular area to make a good decision on the use of technology.

You should make a habit of reading articles you run across related to technology. You may find out all you need to know about your next purchase from a standard write up.

If your business is heavily tech reliant, than obviously you should be subscribed to several high quality magazines.

There may be seminars in your area sponsored by trade organizations, local tech companies or a college that you may contact to learn about existing and future technologies.

There are also freelancers who specialize in helping businesses put together the right technologies to run their operation efficiently; even on a shoestring budget.

Any freelancers worth their salt will advertise on the internet or in local business directories. Local colleges are an excellent resource for you to tap as they will undoubtedly have a tech department and will surely refer you to someone who may be able to help you further.

Go ahead and Google "top 100 emerging tech trends" and you will get your fill of articles; you can also pinpoint the search by narrowing in on a particular area. Get a feel for what is happening in the world around you.

Most of what you see may not apply to you per se, but as a business person, it may be relevant to a customer of yours.

Remember, you are to be a reliable source of information for yourself *and* for your customers. Even if technology is not your strong point, you need to make an effort to be knowledgeable about what is out there and what is on the way.

Even if you are a small business and feel that you are limited, buying the right technology would save you money and make you money in the long run. For instance, a company called Construction Robotics in the U.S., developed a semi-automated mason (SAM) which handles the repetitive & strenuous task of lifting and placing each brick.

Such a product, despite the cost, would surely save time and money for a construction company who would invest in such a purchase as it would replace one or more employees who would have to be paid to do this same job.

You can also automate marketing, which is a necessary tool for even the smallest of businesses. This allows for the reduction of time & effort spent on such tasks.

Drones may help on construction sites and other fields beyond the casual recreation use they have for most of the public currently.

Do your research and do not allow yourself to be intimidated by what you don't know. There is plenty to learn and it all doesn't have to be grasped all in one day! So, take your time and slowly add to your knowledge of emerging technologies!

IN CONCLUSION

WE HOPE YOU ARE ABLE TO USE THIS INFORMATION PROFITABLY AND ENJOY IT IMMENSELY AGAIN AND AGAIN!

PLEASE LET US KNOW HOW YOU FEEL ABOUT THE BOOK; LEAVE A REVIEW!

CONTACT US AT
INDISTRIBUTION@OUTLOOK.COM

www.ingramcontent.com/pod-product-compliance
Lightning Source LLC
Chambersburg PA
CBHW070409190526
45169CB00003B/1182